THE TRANSCONTINENTAL RAILROAD

by **ERIC KRAFT**

Table of Contents

The Need

It was the 1850s. Gold had recently been discovered in California, and people wanted to get there to try their luck at finding some. The United States Army wanted to transport men and materials to fight Native Americans and claim their land in the West for the new country. Settlers wanted to move west to claim land the government offered them free if they settled it and farmed it. Pressure was growing to build a railroad across the country.

At the time, railroads went as far west as the Mississippi and Missouri rivers. The United States extended far beyond, across the Great Plains, the Rocky Mountains, and the Sierra Nevada Mountains to the Pacific Ocean.

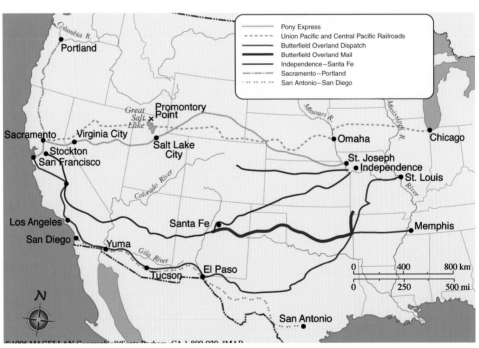

▲ In 1850, there were few wagon trails available for overland travel. By 1870, these major rail and stagecoach routes existed.

Railroads were the most modern form of transportation at the time. They were faster, more comfortable, and more reliable than other means available.

Without a railroad to California, travelers from the East Coast had a choice of three routes—all of them long and dangerous. They could sail by ship around South America. That journey took them through stormy weather and violent seas.

They could sail by ship to Panama. There they had to cross the country by canoe, mule, horse, or on foot. Then they had to board a ship to California. There was always great danger of disease.

Their third choice was the land route across the United States. The trails were rugged and the weather was fierce. There was constant danger of disease or attack by Native Americans.

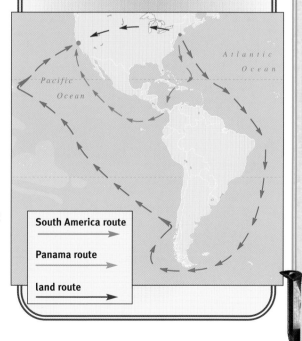

Atlantic Ocean

Pacific Ocean

South America route

Panama route

land route

By 1861, the need for a railroad across the country was great. President Abraham Lincoln was eager to have such a railroad built. Businesspeople wanted it, too. If so many people supported the construction of a **transcontinental** railroad, why wasn't one being built?

The construction of a railroad across the country needed the approval of Congress. Much of the land that would be used belonged to the federal government.

The northern states were arguing with the southern states about the route the railroad should take. The railroad would bring economic development, so the northern states wanted it to follow a northern route and the southern states wanted a southern route. Congress couldn't agree on a **compromise** (KOM-pruh-myz).

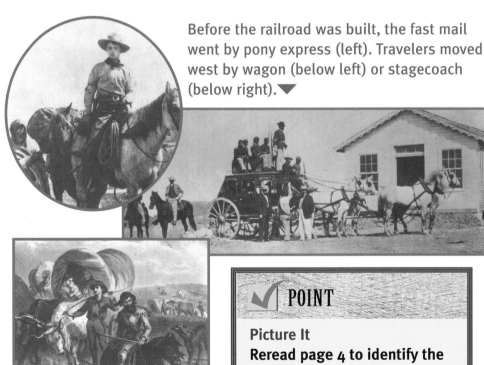

Before the railroad was built, the fast mail went by pony express (left). Travelers moved west by wagon (below left) or stagecoach (below right). ▼

✔ POINT

Picture It
Reread page 4 to identify the problem between the North and the South.

There were also strong social, economic, and political differences between the North and the South. The critical issue of slavery was at the heart of those differences.

The South's economy was based mainly on agriculture. Thus the South depended heavily on its 4 million black slaves. Because slaves were so important to its economy, the South was committed to continuing the practice of slavery.

The North had developed more manufacturing industries. It was also home to the nation's largest banks. When Abraham Lincoln was elected president in 1860, he was opposed to slavery. States in the South decided to withdraw, or **secede** (si-SEED), from the Union. Within months, the North and the South were at war.

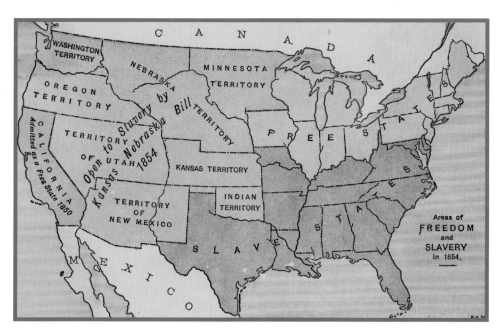

▲ At the start of the Civil War, the United States was divided by the issue of slavery.

When the southern states seceded, there were no longer any votes in Congress for a southern railroad route. In 1862, Congress authorized the Central Pacific Railroad to build from Sacramento, California, east and the Union Pacific Railroad to build from Omaha, Nebraska, west. Much of the intended routes followed an old pioneer trail.

The two routes that the railroad would follow had been discovered by teams led by two adventurous **surveyors** (ser-VAY-erz). Grenville Dodge had led a team that mapped the Union Pacific's route. Theodore Judah had found a route from San Francisco through the Sierra Nevada Mountains that the Central Pacific would follow.

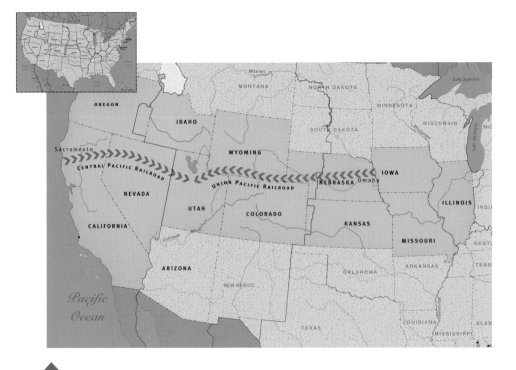

The Central Pacific Railroad was to extend east from Sacramento, California. The Union Pacific Railroad was to be built from Omaha, Nebraska, west.

Building the transcontinental railroad would cost a great deal of money. The federal government was willing to help. Congress agreed to lend the railroads $16,000 (about $208,000 in today's dollars) for every mile of track they laid on flat land, $32,000 ($416,000) for every mile of track they laid on plateaus, and $48,000 ($624,000) for every mile of track they laid in the mountains. The government would also give the railroads 6,400 acres for every mile of track they laid. In 1864, Congress doubled the amount of land it gave the railroads. The railroads were free to sell this land or use it as they wished.

IT'S A FACT!

Grenville Dodge

Theodore Judah

Grenville Dodge personally surveyed the route the Union Pacific would follow all the way from Omaha through the Platte Valley, over the Rockies, to the Great Salt Lake in Utah. Dodge later became the chief engineer for the Union Pacific.

Theodore Judah personally surveyed the route the Central Pacific would follow through the Sierra Nevada Mountains. He camped for months under the worst conditions while he looked for the best pass through the mountains. After surveying, he spent years trying to convince the government that the railroad should be built.

The Obstacles

Both railroads faced many problems. The cost would be enormous. They would have to go over or through the tallest mountain ranges on the continent. They would have to work in winter blizzards and desert heat.

Work on the Central Pacific started in 1863, but it got off to a slow start. The route eastward from Sacramento ran into the Sierra Nevada Mountains almost immediately. The workers had to wind their way up the mountains. They couldn't go straight up and over because the **grade**, or slope, of the track would have been too steep. No **locomotive** could have climbed it. As a result, only 50 miles of track were laid in the first two years.

▲ a view of Sacramento, California, when work on the Central Pacific began

The Union Pacific started work in 1865. The workers began building on the flat land of the Great Plains. They could clear land, grade it, and lay track across it far faster there than in mountainous areas. For them, the Rocky Mountains lay ahead, toward the end of their work.

The railroad was laying track through Native American lands. The company's cooks were killing buffalo to feed the work crews. This angered the Native Americans, who depended on buffalo for food, clothing, and tools.

Native Americans also objected to the fact that the railroad line would split the buffalo grazing lands of the plains in two. In many ways the railroad would ruin the Native American way of life. So the Native Americans attacked the crews, burned supplies, and tore up track.

☞ IT'S A FACT!

When work on the railroad began in 1863, about 60 million buffalo were living on the Great Plains. Settlers and railroad crews killed many buffalo for sport, for their hides, and sometimes for food. By the end of the 1800s, fewer than 1,000 buffalo were left.

This 1862 illustration depicts buffalo hunting, an important part of Native American life on the prairie.

Both the Central Pacific and the Union Pacific had to battle the weather. In springtime, rains and floods washed out bridges and sections of track. The winters were even worse. On the plains and in the mountains, snow driven by high winds covered the tracks so deeply that even the largest locomotives couldn't get through.

There was an added danger in the mountains — **avalanches** (AV-uh-lanch-ez).

An avalanche is a sudden collapse and slide of piled-up snow. The Central Pacific eventually built sheds over the tracks to protect them from avalanches. Although the sheds were built of wood, they were strong enough to support the weight of the snow. One shed stretched for 28 miles.

Snow slowed the work and threatened regular railroad traffic. ▼

Transporting necessary equipment was a problem for both companies, but especially for the Central Pacific. Most of its supplies had to be shipped from the East Coast around South America to California. This was a long and dangerous route for the heavy lengths of track, the explosive powder used to blast tunnels through the mountains, and the various locomotives and cars.

POINT

Picture It
Reread page 10. Close your eyes and picture railroad tracks with a shed covering them. Draw what you see and share your picture with a friend.

▲ Locomotive parts from the East were delivered by steamship to the Central Pacific's Sacramento wharf. When the ship docked, timber and rail would be unloaded onto the wharf.

The Union Pacific, building from east to west, had an easier time at first. It could ship supplies along its own railroad track as it was laid. Even so, the job was enormous. Not only did the company have to build a railroad, it had to house and feed all its workers.

As the railroad pushed farther into the wilderness, both supplies and workers had to be transported. It was as if a town of 10,000 workers were slowly traveling across America, bringing all its needs with it.

At the outset, conditions favored the Union Pacific over the Central Pacific. Because the Union Pacific route went across plains and through mountains with wide passes, the Union Pacific was able to lay more track faster than the Central Pacific.

▼ Railroad workers lived in camp-like conditions up and down the railroad line.

Central Pacific workers had to blast through granite mountains in the Sierra Nevada range to build 15 tunnels. Sometimes they advanced only eight inches a day, while the Union Pacific moved miles ahead each day.

The Central Pacific also had trouble keeping workers. Men would join the work crew but stay just long enough to reach the gold fields of California. Or they would work just long enough to earn the money to buy supplies, and then they would run off in search of gold.

Both companies decided to build as fast as they could rather than try to make the work perfect. They would fix or replace what had to be fixed or replaced later. But the railroad had to be built first.

✔ POINT

Think It Over

When the railroad tunnel under the English Channel was built in the 1990s, 11 huge tunneling machines did the work of digging. They were guided by laser beams to make sure they stayed on course.

The 15 tunnels that the Central Pacific built were dug by hand. One steam-driven shovel was tried briefly, but it was not effective. Workers dug the Summit Tunnel in the Sierra Nevadas, just northwest of Lake Tahoe, from both ends. When they met in the middle, they were only three inches off course!

What is the author's purpose for including the first paragraph?

The Workers

At the height of railroad construction, about 20,000 people were working on the transcontinental railroad. At the start of the project, Union Pacific workers were mostly Irish **immigrants** (IM-uh-grents). They were joined by Germans, English, and Mexicans. These immigrants had left their native homes in search of a better life in America. When the Civil War ended, veterans and former slaves joined the work crews.

The owners of the company were careless about paying their workers. Often the men went without pay for long periods of time. Meanwhile, the owners were making fortunes from government loans and land grants.

▲ Managers had to organize the work of huge crews of workers along each railroad line.

The Union Pacific workers lived in railroad cars. As the railroad advanced westward, the company set up a supply camp every 70 miles or so. Some of these camps became towns we know today, such as Cheyenne and Laramie, Wyoming. The supply camps were often violent and lawless places, without government, police, or courts.

▲ Supply camps, such as this one, sometimes grew into towns and cities.

The first teams of workers were survey crews. They worked far ahead of the track layers, marking the route that the railroad would follow. They were like explorers, camping in the outdoors.

Behind the surveyors came the grading teams. They leveled the land and sloped it so that the track would follow a path locomotives could climb. They worked with picks, shovels, and wheelbarrows to cut the tops from hills and fill valleys, making uneven ground smooth and level enough for railroad tracks.

After the graders came the teams that set the wooden **ties** in place. The ties were cross pieces that would hold the steel rails. When they could, these teams cut trees and shaped the ties on the spot.

▲ This construction camp of the Central Pacific railroad was set up in 1869 in Utah. It was home to the various teams of workers.

The last teams were the track layers. A horse-drawn cart loaded with rails would come speeding along the track that had already been laid. As it did, men from the track teams would lift rails off the cart from both sides, run forward with them, and drop them in place. Then they would run right back for more rails. Other men would swarm into position and begin pounding spikes into the rails to hold them in place on the ties. By the time these men had finished driving spikes, the rail carriers had dropped the next rails in place. Everyone would run forward to the next position and the process would continue. Workers called the sound of hammers ringing on steel rails the "Anvil Chorus."

▲ Workers drove every spike by hand in a manner similar to that used by a more modern railroad worker.

✓ POINT

Talk About It
Many workers were injured during the building of the railroad, and many were killed. No one knows just how many, because the railroad companies did not keep records of their accidents.
With a group member, talk about the dangers the workers faced.

The Central Pacific dealt with the problem of workers deserting for the gold fields by hiring Chinese immigrants. Eventually, almost 9,000 of the 10,000 Central Pacific workers were Chinese. Most of them were already living in California. They had come there for the same reason other people had—they were hoping to make their fortunes in the gold fields. However, California laws **discriminated** (dis-KRIM-uh-nated) against them, preventing them from making as much money as prospectors. Therefore, they needed work and found it on the railroad. Chinese workers on the Central Pacific had to blast their way through mountains to lay track. They did this by drilling holes in the granite and filling them with explosive powder.

Chinese workers dug most of the Central Pacific's tunnels. They had already helped build the California Central and San Jose railroads. ▼

They drilled the powder holes by hand because they had no power drills. One worker would hold a steel drill against the rock and another would hit the drill with a heavy iron hammer. Many workers lost fingers or hands when a hammer missed its mark.

In some situations, a worker would be lowered down the face of a cliff in a basket. He would push black powder into the cliff and light it. Then he would be pulled up before the explosion occurred.

Workers on the Union Pacific started out laying one mile of track a day on flat land. They improved to eight miles a day. When the Central Pacific workers got past the Sierra Nevadas and reached level land, they laid a record 10 miles of track in a single day. It was all done by hand.

A sign marks the spot where Central Pacific workers laid 10 miles of track in a single day.

The Golden Spike

Originally, Congress had instructed the Central Pacific to stop laying track at the border of California and Nevada, where the Union Pacific would meet it. Later, Congress changed the rule by allowing the Central Pacific to keep advancing eastward until it met the Union Pacific.

A race to lay the most track, and thereby get more money and land, was on! Newspapers picked up the story and people followed it excitedly.

Surveyors for each railroad had already marked where the track should be laid. The graders following them were working as fast as possible to prepare the way for the track layers. Unfortunately, Congress had not indicated exactly where the two railroads should

meet. So the grading teams met but continued to grade past each other for hundreds of miles. Because no one knew which company would lay its track faster, each grading team wanted the grade ready if its company should be the winner.

Congress realized that this was a waste of effort and money. It decided that the two sets of tracks should meet at Promontory Point, Utah.

In the interest of speed, the Union Pacific built its bridges of wood, planning to replace them with iron once the railroad was completed. ▼

☞ IT'S A FACT!

In 1863, when work on the railroad was just getting under way, George Pullman designed a railroad sleeping car. It had seats that could be pulled out to become beds, or berths. Above them, upper berths unfolded from the walls. In 1867, Pullman started the Pullman Palace Car Company, which built sleeping cars and dining cars.

On May 10, 1869, engines from the two railroads met at Promontory Point. They came so close together that they actually touched.

Central Pacific's engine, Jupiter, was a wood-burning engine. Most of the Central Pacific engines burned wood, because wood was plentiful in the forests along the route of the Central Pacific.

Union Pacific's Engine 119 was a coal-burner. It was fired by coal from the east, which the Union Pacific could easily transport along its own railroad as it moved westward. It would have cost the Central Pacific a fortune to ship that coal to the West Coast.

When the tracks from the two railroads met, the race was over. The Central Pacific had laid 689 miles of track. The Union Pacific had laid 1,086 miles of track.

To celebrate the completion of the railroad, the governor of California, Leland Stanford, planned to drive a golden spike into the ties where the two railroads met. Engineers had attached a telegraph wire to the spike. When the spike was struck by a hammer, the sound would be sent to New York, San Francisco, and all the cities and towns in between. The entire nation would know about the event at the precise moment it happened.

Mission accomplished! The last rail was laid and the golden spike was driven at Promontory Point, Utah, on May 10, 1869. ▼

▲ The golden spike was to be driven into the ties where the Union Pacific and Central Pacific railroads met at Promontory Point, Utah.

Stanford swung a special silver hammer at the golden spike—and missed! He hit the rail instead. But the sound went out over the telegraph line, and the nation sent up a cheer.

People celebrated from coast to coast. Bells rang in churches and town halls.

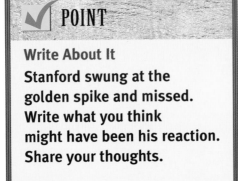

POINT

Write About It
Stanford swung at the golden spike and missed. Write what you think might have been his reaction. Share your thoughts.

Even the Liberty Bell was rung. Of course, it was rung very carefully because it had cracked in 1835. No one wanted to crack it further.

The golden spike really was made of gold. Its head was engraved with the words "THE LAST SPIKE." After the ceremony, it was removed from the tie and replaced with an ordinary spike. Today, the golden spike is on display at Stanford University in Palo Alto, California.

Years earlier, when workers on the Central Pacific were about to drive their first spike, one of the owners wanted to celebrate the occasion. Another owner, Collis Huntington, advised against it. "If you want to jubilate over driving the first spike," he wrote, "go ahead and do it. I don't. Those mountains over there look too ugly [difficult]. . . . Anybody can drive the first spike, but there are many months of labor and unrest between the first and last spike."

He was right about the months of labor and hardship. But the railroad had been built. The mountains had been crossed. The last spike had been driven.

THE PACIFIC RAILWAY.

Exercises Attending the Laying of the Last Rail at Promontory, Utah —Presentation of a Silver Spike— The Last Tie—Speeches and Despatches.

PROMONTORY, Utah, Tuesday, May 11.—In presenting the silver spike to Dr. Durant yesterday, in performance of his part in the exercises attending the laying of the last rail of the great Pacific Road, Hon. T. A. Tuttle, of Nevada, offered the following sentiment:

To the iron of the East and the gold of the West, Nevada adds her link of silver to span the Continent and wed the oceans.

Hon. A. K. Safford, Governor of Arizona, offered a spike of iron, silver, and gold, as an offering from

▲ This article appeared in *The World* newspaper, published in New York City on May 12, 1869.

The Results

The transcontinental railroad was completed in six years—eight years ahead of schedule! Its total cost, while difficult to determine exactly, has been estimated at $125 million, which would be $1.6 billion today.

The actual route of the transcontinental railroad differed from the planned route. Difficulties in laying track had made **detours** (DEE-toorz) necessary.

▼ In addition to showing the route of the Central Pacific, this map provided the distances between and the altitudes of major stops on the route.

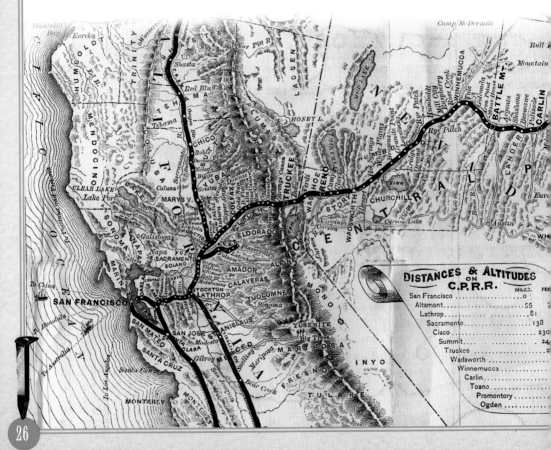

DISTANCES & ALTITUDES ON C.P.R.R.

	MILES.	FEE
San Francisco	0	
Altamont	55	
Lathrop	81	
Sacramento	138	
Cisco	230	
Summit	24	
Truckee		
Wadsworth		
Winnemucca		
Carlin		
Toano		
Promontory		
Ogden		

Sometimes an easier way to cross a river had to be found. Sometimes following a pass through mountains made building easier, even if the route might be a few miles longer.

Critics of the Union Pacific said that some of the railroad's detours were not necessary. They accused the managers of going out of their way to build more miles of track to get more government money and land.

Posters and newspaper ads announced transcontinental service.

Over the course of building the transcontinental railroad, the Union Pacific and Central Pacific became the two biggest corporations in the country. The people who had financed the railroads from the start recognized that there were two ways to make money. They could make money by building the railroad, and they could make money by running it.

POINT

Think It Over

Imagine that all the people in the United States weighed the same. Also imagine that you could balance the country on a stick the way a juggler balances a spinning plate. The center of population is the point where the country would balance perfectly. The map below shows the center of population. Why do you think the center of population took a big leap to the west after the transcontinental railroad opened?

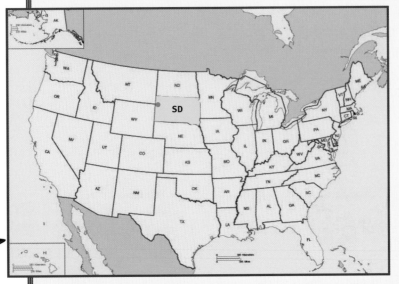

This map shows the current center of population in the United States.

When Theodore Judah began the Central Pacific, he was primarily interested in the railroad itself. He believed in the benefits it would bring as the fastest means of available transportation. The people he found to finance the railroad in its early days, before the government money began rolling in, came to be called the "Big Four." They were Leland Stanford, Collis Huntington, Charles Crocker, and Mark Hopkins. They all made enormous sums of money.

The heads of the Union Pacific were Thomas Durant, Congressman Oakes Ames, and Oliver Ames. Like the "Big Four" of the Central Pacific, Durant and the Ames brothers put up the money to get the railroad started before government money was available.

IT'S A FACT!

Railroads changed the way people kept track of time. Before the railroads were built, each community kept its own time, which was a little bit different from the time in the next community. The railroads needed a standard time so that schedules of train arrivals and departures could be published. The four standard time zones in the United States were instituted.

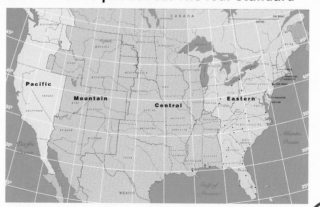

▲ This map shows the time zones in the United States. In which time zone do you live?

The transcontinental railroad opened the West to many more people. Travel across the country was not only faster, but much cheaper and safer. People could travel across the country to visit family and friends or to seek new places to settle and new opportunities to explore.

The railroad also helped people think of the United States as one country stretching "from sea to shining sea." The country was huge and its distances vast, but the railroad had shrunk those distances. Because the crews had strung a telegraph line alongside the railroad as they built it, people could stay in touch even when they were far away. Cheap and easy travel along with rapid communication knit the nation together.

▼ The transcontinental railroad made the transport of people and goods easier. It also helped settle the West.

Glossary

avalanche **(AV-uh-lanch) a sudden collapse of piled-up snow** (page 10)

compromise **(KOM-pruh-myz) a settlement of differences reached by consent of all** (page 4)

detour **(DEE-toor) a route different from the planned one** (page 26)

discriminate **(dis-KRIM-uh-nate) to treat someone unfairly because of race, sex, or ethnic group** (page 18)

grade **(GRAYD) the slope or incline of a stretch of land** (page 8)

immigrant **(IM-uh-grent) a person who comes to live in a country from another country, usually hoping for a better life** (page 14)

locomotive **(LO-ke-MO-tiv) an engine used to pull or push railroad cars along a track** (page 8)

secede **(si-SEED) to withdraw from an organized group** (page 5)

surveyor **(ser-VAY-er) a person who lays out boundaries or routes on land** (page 6)

tie **(TY) a cross piece, usually wood, on which railroad rails are laid** (page 16)

transcontinental **(TRANZ-kon-tin-EN-tel) crossing an entire continent** (page 4)

Index